PASSING MEASURES

PETER RILEY

PASSING MEASURES

A Collection of Poems

CARCANET

First published in 2000 by
Carcanet Press Limited
4th Floor, Conavon Court
12–16 Blackfriars Street
Manchester M3 5BQ

A CIP catalogue record for this book
is available from the British Library

ISBN 1 85754 485 4

The publisher acknowledges financial assistance
from the Arts Council of England

Set in Monotype Garamond by XL Publishing Services, Tiverton
Printed and bound in England by SRP Ltd, Exeter

The defenceless men and women with nothing but common beauty. The passionate and the passionless. The obdurate heart, and the little piping, brittle one. The bristling mind hiccuping with ideas, and the dull one, a flat plain under the black arc of an empty skull.

Jack B. Yeats, *The Amaranthers* (1936)

Contents

I. KING'S FIELD

Material Soul   13
Prelude   14
Wandering Voices   14
Patina   15
Ballad of the Broken Bridge   15
Pause at Harecops   18
Driving down the Wye and Stopping   18
Driving up the Erewash and Arriving   19
Cavendish Cottages   20
No Sweet Dream   21
Distant Point   22
Greenwich Marshes and All the Way Home   22
Tumulus   23
Paws at Harecops   24
from Thirty Poems of Ten Lines   24

II. SEA WATCHES

II. SEA WATCHES   31
     SEA WATCH ELEGIES   47
     BETWEEN HARBOURS   52

III. OSPITA

III. OSPITA   57

IV. *from* NOON PROVINCE

Arriving at Dawn   67
Market Day   67
Roofwatch   68
Meditations in the Fields   69
Lines at the Pool above St.-Saturnin   70
Escape from our Uncaring   71
Lacoste   72
Recalling Lacoste   72
Counting the Cost (Syllables at Night)   73
Up the Big Hill and Back by Ten   74

Resolution and Interdependence 75
Real Number 75
Just a Song 76
Stating the Case 77
The Telephone Box on the Edge of the Cornfield 77
Last Night 78
Orange to Chartres 81
Slow Meditation 82

V. SELECTED POEMS 1966–1996

1966–1970
Urizon 87
A Column of Air 88
Valley of the Moon 89
from The Linear Journal 89
In a German Car-park 92
Bunker Hotel 93
Is This Dusseldorf or Kiel? 94
Four Night Pacts 95
Folded Message 96
Grassy Lenses 96
1976–1990
Clouds and Birds over Wolfscote 97
Boletus Under Narrowdale 97
Prelude 98
Further Education 98
Poem Beginning with a Line by Nicholas Moore 99
Bole Hill 99
Little Bolehill 100
Midsummer Common 100
Dublin 101
Loft 101
Hackney Loft 102
Parker's Piece 102
Three Roman Churches
S. Cecilia in Trastevere 103
S. Maria in Trastevere 103
S. Pietro in Montorio 104
Three Poems in Tunisia
Djebel Bou Dabbous 104

Djebel Bou Dabbous   105
Ghar El Melh   106
Three Parts of Paris
Saint Séverin's Maze   107
Causeway   107
Pascal's Corner   108
Poems from the trilogy Reader – Lecture – Author
I. Reader
Bolehill   109
Hastings   109
Irish Drones   110
Golden Slumbers   110
II. Lecture
Vallée de la Vézère   111
Glow Worm True Worm   112
Heinrich Biber   112
Magdelanian   113
III. Author
In Manus Tuas   113
'Voiced consonants…'   114
Do It Again   115
Bar Carol   116
'And love alone…'   116
Poems to Paintings by Jack B. Yeats
Prelude: Night Shift   117
Oh My Beauty!   118
Men of Destiny   119
The Stolen Picture   119
The Little Watercolour at Sligo   120
That Grand Conversation Was Under the Rose   120

Bibliography   123

I

KING'S FIELD

A selection from the Peak District writings, 1974–1985

Material Soul

Given to death and life, no choice,
fallen into these terms, born as the
tide bears the wave to its strike,
cut to bedrock, crest, charge the shore.
Given to this life carving itself out
of its knowledge and the earth
is a cup to which the lip fits, then
surely the senses' final construct
moves through substance to the houses
of light, mutual devotion

joined to death; danger
specifies its fear, the message forms
its own access or nerve and behind
the point of contact perception opens
onto a cleared space, a settlement, holding
people of all ages together –
the whole of life, is this shift
back, this rearing

and arrival, which leaves a mark,
a birth documentation or yell echoing
down the unliveable corridors and arcades
of transitional time. Flesh scores lines
in the calcium slag of earth and the spirit
wakes, the needle enters the groove,
polar tension shakes the circuit, which
responds, gapes, tremors, issues
forth into the acts of day, for good.
Peace is nothing without this resistance,
engaging distance beyond any possible
repair to the end, the inhabited city.

Prelude

Each day some further light each day some farther dark.
Carry on go here there make a note of it what for.
Climb the hill walk down get in the car and drive away.
It is nothing to do with me. Valley stream
meadow waterfall gorge. There is something else there
nothing to do with us, that makes no difference.
We can go we can stay at home and drink tea, it is
still there. Far reaches of the Upper Manifold, where
is it, what is it, green chapel if it rains it rains.
Smear of cloud in the distance, book of nothing not
inhabited, ruins of the whole thing. Light on water
quick by blue shale cliffs, thick in fern, light filling,
bearing the vocabulary of a curved lack. Mineral vein
running down the hillside up the other side and away
over the moors, worked or not. Or not worked, unknown,
what difference does that make? Light filling the valley
with not a soul to be seen, dark beams of disappointment
filling the city streets, death shadowing the grass.
What am I then as you which otherwise stays sleeping, or
if we weren't in the dark star's way would our sense
still track the earth whether we knew it or not?
No, the material soul yearns by the day's annoyance for real.
So does love in silver boxes hence despatch our joyful stake
and I turn us again, front to front to front.

Wandering Voices

Night outside is the theatre of our patience
as you lie beside me in the dark loft,
distant thrust of steam locomotive in some
vast marshalling yard, cold papers blown
across the square.

Night contracts the distances of love and fortune
to a presence, angles filling the dark room
loud with inaudible instructions like an
equestrian statue in the full moon and a far away
telephone rings.

It is me trying to contact a third person
out of the past or lost in the city streets while
night's cover persists — footsteps of the heart agent
passing by ticket office and clock tower
to an abandoned station.

Then false dawn brings a nil invoice and faint lines
near the ceiling, a small child runs down the corridor
holding a toy angel, wings flapping, screaming at us
not to owe — the world is wanted, and full, our full hearts
crack at it.

And famine of the earth in pictorial wars, false
tensions, monetarisation of time whereas the emptiness
is real and there is no return, no restitution
oh keep intact the underwing starts, the
cup through it.

Patina

Willing also to be remembered, lost
in fairest love-task scholarships such
as bring sight to its own predilection
where the broken edges catch the light
in sequence, a tract where sense
and love fuse in the energy of script
holding the world together at that point.

And an immense wastage, entirely ours
as we humanise the world and then resent it
objectify it and wonder where it's gone
and place such limits on our acts that
most of the people become figments of something
shot past like a disintegrated pudding too late for
winter, the fields rationalised to dust.

But I also think of you as fairest before sight
in a vocabulary which is generally considered
nonsense out of a 13th Century context and still
fairer dark by the light that glims beyond.
Well, it is night at the crossroads and many years
since a dignitary came this way. The faces
of the houses are silent. Time suddenly rusts.

Ballad of the Broken Bridge

If you want messages you must provide an orifice.
But to really want messages is in itself an orifice,
a lesion, an interruption of the diurnal pact. The future
ferments in this cleft, packed with honour and disdain,
drawing us ever larger and further on, to this self-
same world, that listens; the rest is vain stuff.

Surely it is this whole particular, this action we
are that draws our sight into the funnel, opening
and closing as the light wing flutters, back
and forth, back and forth, wisdom and rubbish –
poetry is the flight. And now if I can just get out
of this notional claw I'll find out exactly where I am.

> I'm in the dining shed again exactly up and about
> my morning task I crawl at this morning through
> the floss of dream. In a wink I fill the kettle
> and forget it. I shake the radio. I wince.
> The light outside is clearer than any hypothesis.
> The edge resounds in light because we don't linger.

And off to work I go. I enter a solid block
of morning light scored with branch lines;
I close the door before you even wake, check
ignition and brakes and turn again to the book,
to the page shewn, the passage marked before.
Fate, it says, is a professional improvisor.

I duck under the brow as the overtakers
glide past in their dream wagons: Monday
Tuesday and Wednesday, fleeces thick in oil.
Feeling 'rushed' (like 'crowded') mounts to
a signal. I turn into a lay-by with herbage. Rain
clouds the stream. The entire landscape is vocal.

I lean on the parapet while the police matrons
check my documentation, and listen to the story
of the water vole, his home under the bridge, the pain
of his extended incisors. He breathes under Saturn
and scurries along the bank. He eats or is taken – he
knows that. His duties end at his honour to himself.

We have considerable doubts, but raise a song
of this inadequacy the thrush couldn't fault.
And we keep it, chuck it over the shoulder for
luck and resume direction. A mended stone.
Nothing any longer bears on us that isn't ours;
nothing any longer wears us that isn't love.

Hell in some century's language is where no one
makes a life any more. We have the key to it, fast
to the wrist under the sleeve, the misplaced heart.
Then we mine into light in a way no office can
endure or regulate save the office of delight,
past and future safe in a shell and love's farther still.

Pause at Harecops

The light (this
morning) falls out of the sky
and passes into the ground
and the stone and slate of the roof,

falls into heat
and number
at substance, where
shadows contrive

and the rising penumbra
intercepts
this divine speed
ay at the forge of lives.

Driving down the Wye and Stopping

The light alternates, comes and goes
in days and years and yet remains
the perfection of constancy held in
the length of terrain by human sight.

The streams descend from the hills and
gather towards the plain, broaden and
deepen in the lower valleys, sun's
face cast in their shifting surfaces

playing gently back to the side walls
of terraced houses, stone sheds, slowly
decaying factories: sites of persistence
toil and comfort held in the flickering light

of which nothing is left but the record
that we make of it all, an enduring thing
compacted of energy and substance, and anchor
the language to a history of completions.

For what is trustworthy in this world
but the heartfold, the construct that endures
beyond our means, the weight and stability
of the living transcript as the last light stalls.

Driving up the Erewash and Arriving

To see one thing clearly we distort
the entire landscape: it bends, clouds,
dissolves and slips away to a darkness
out of time; and the one thing being known
at once radiates back its own illumination,
splaying up the cleft towards day.

The landscape is fed back to its source
at our fingertips; the one thing being made
crawls up the ladder towards home,
redoubling the truth of what there is,
by what there surely must be. Catch and
keep it as a caution of the mind

that moves on the surface of earth
day by day in a strict veracity
to which the light responds, playing
and diversifying its facets among
the town roofs and windbreaks –
the script of light on the fields

and houses articulating the true
wish for peace as a space to which
everyone has perfect right of access
and of reward in return for care.
And the profit to the generality.
Such is the simple tale of light

that spreads over the meadows and estates
every morning, rears itself aloft
and late in the day slides sideways away
off the pointed roofs and hedge backs
it flows, and slips away, never
(in a way) to return, since we are mortal.

Cavendish Cottages

And what if we endured earth's glory
outside the museum, outside the silence
what if we bought something of the world
worth more than a Welcome doormat?
And what if we take the pain
as a factor of resistance and
continue, under the three protectors:
road, food, house.

> The old man sits by the gas fire, cat
> on knee, fixed to the portable T.V.
> All his knowledge is constantly averted
> until there is hardly anything left
> but a cancelled claim, and the masters of silence
> talk unanswerably in a luminous blue mist
> beamed at the soul's shell. So his dream
> passes constantly, wider and wider
> through him, and will, until there's ´
> nothing left, poor ghost.

And what if we endure
the glory of earth's pain
anywhere, loudly,
dazzled by the actual world
articulating light
in the eye.

And fold the heartspace
back to protecting source.
And get off our backs and lend a hand.

No Sweet Dream

Nobody's writing The Phenomenology of Evil.
Stay awake and keep talking, fill the space
with substance, like an Irish brooch, draw out
the ribbon, fold and wind it into the enclosure,
which is the house, which means communication.
Draw it from the world's persistence. Tonight's
parcel post like a lion in the forest moves
to expectation, to continuity and response
and what if perfectly solid men, men without
compassion, insurrect between us, toiling to
block the line with hollow gain – Nobody's writing
The Phenomenology of Evil and a moment's honesty
clears all the space we've got.

And nobody's writing the phenomenology of evil because
nobody wants to know. Each day the darkness shuts earlier
and behind the houses in old yards and neglected allotments
moths hover in clouds of seed under the arch of nettles
a warm fermenting vapour holds the night creatures in ecstasy
as by day the martens zoom over the stubble fields
in great ellipses darting between electricity wires
and again the earth is caught in full action, engaged against
its own inertia and which side could we possibly be on?
We continue not writing the phenomenology of evil because
we can't be bothered, because our brain cells decay too fast,
because we still have the space available of a more urgent
engagement with good, knowing that no one will ever write
The Phenomenology of Evil because, set in the outering vortex
we view it and there's no one there; it's a cloud of
husk-powder in the eye between two walls, a television
cut, there's not a soul to be seen.

Distant Point

And the saint on his tiny island in the lake
like a doctor in his surgery, islanded off
from the unhealing world and blasted out
of self regard by force of work – love
like this meets constantly the resistance of
matter directly as a gardener where every shrub
is won from nothing into the ancestral shield,
and the stones rise to the hand.

Greenwich Marshes and All the Way Home

The city's surface and perimeter swollen
with lights, command of feeling as extended
and productive biological need, 5 police cars
and an ambulance. The slightest immediate
kindly act and the very gaucheness to say it.

The catalogues of favour slowly accumulate
in right acts of any scale, etymologies and
histories of musical instruments, whether in
rage or cheer we burn through the night of thought
until the flags descend on us.

All the work is directed to this grace
whereby in a moment's turn as in a year's
bulletin we are rehumoured, and cast
resentment adrift like a fishing line
in the earth's blackness behind our home.

Oh lightly as if not bothered, to justify
being this forward transaction between soil & sky
that sharpens its claws on the city walls
and laughs at the tortuous blinds of earth,
knows them to a T and adores the green patina.

Then as the candle burns lower the spoils
of chaos are set in a wicker basket and brought
to market, bearing his fatherly self for smelting,
and courage is care, care is purpose, the weight
of earth falls off.

Tumulus

Sparks of flesh scattered on the earth,
flowers, that speculate, and call and call
till there is no rest to be had, the tower flats
buzzing and flashing through the night beside the river,

Procession of tail-lights on the motorway arm,
tunnel of orange glow, sweeping past the spangled
power stations and depots, clouds of steam lit inter-
mittently from below, brief flowers on a tumulus.

We are worn to a point in the clarified dark,
flesh smoke always in our nostrils and before
our eyes sharpening the distance towards the end,
the island home and true response

For in spite of everything we are together,
every single one of us, dead and alive,
and something won't let us forget it, this
endless hammering inside matter.

Paws at Harecops

Full moon, limestone ridge
a grey bank against the night sky,

Aura in the trees and round
the corners of the house, not a

Match struck. The mouse
squeaks in the grass,

The cat sleeps, dreaming
tomorrow into question.

The mines – they all ended
in a silent lake.

from *Thirty Poems of Ten Lines*

2)

All that happened
and where's the poem of it?
– there in your surface speaking
your body writing your soul

tall
and never still
like the autumn grass

we could happen to
a Lycian double music
conjugates my throat weft

3) *for Stephen*

Your mother left you in care
Maybe she didn't care
Who now is to care
for and about you —

that you manage,
and have to bear
these dreadful puns

and cruel rhyme
since they
drive their cares

8)

Six hours into night and I'm nearly what?
20, 40-what? and what persists —
space, stars, and the singing.

What do the bookshelves care if we
reckon a loss, what does the town
conclude? And further on is what else —

Space, stars, and the track
the rider makes in the sand
singing difficulties and durations
into holes, is that us?

11)

Here out of my writing
your fingertips glow in the darkness
you climb into the valley

and I know my life can never be translated
out of this miserable little hole
full of novels and possibilities –
the very sides of it cut my hands.

On the hard rocks of the heart vale
our sight ends. The magpie moth
lays her eggs in the wound.

16)

From Liverpool to Leeds
a bonfire thrown on a motorway,
a bridge of fire.

For a white smile, for a coated neck
we have razed dignity from our homes.

Your excellent teeth and the light down
on the back of your neck I shall remember
as long as I live. We rivet our time
on happy needs but then overseek – oh it's not
ours to question, we surely are to answer,
surely, to enunciate, arching flame.

17)

It's awful – there are owls and townships in the night
and I'm trembling because some Sales Manager
said 'Now look here…' on the phone.

No resolution is anticipated.
The owl, swooping over, looks ahead;
the town sucks vision down its lamps,
I quarry into night a day's end.

Perhaps it's just that after so much
rooting in humanity
we need something to dry our hands on.

26) *Lesson, after Philippe Jaccottet*

At one time
I, frightened, ignorant, hardly alive,
covering my eyes with images,
claimed to guide the living and the dead.

I, sheltered poet,
set aside, hardly suffering,
dared to trace paths in the abyss.

Now, lamp blown out,
hand more errant and trembling,
I start again slowly in the draught.

30)

One thing
always only

pen on table / gathered evening

one thing wished and
one thing worth it

seedfract / matchless / gathering light

heartbeknown.

II

SEA WATCHES
SEA WATCH ELEGIES
BETWEEN HARBOURS

Llŷn / Peak District / Cambridge 1977–1996

Sea Watches

I. CLIFF-TOP ANNUALS

1
Almost there we hesitate, and turn, high on the soft
Edge of Britain, to view the whole story: the sea barking
Up both sides of the peninsula to the point, top
Crest of land, pilgrims' goal or final extent
Of a life's coming and going called together when
There is after all a focus, an intellectual love.

2
That we shall not reach today and is quite
Obviously already all we are, and warns us
Not to postpone the issue for a quiet bed
Or any other future. The car gentle as a hearse
Takes sunken roads through fields that carry
Sea-glow, yellow scatter, proud, tall and thin.

3
Grey concrete road down old stream cleft
To the bay, white sand, slab sea, guard dog barking,
Chug of generator engine at the beach shop:
Unchanged items. And the same us with different
Surfaces, year after year we are here again.
Alternatim to eternity, if our love is proven.

4
Wide and bright sea spread in the great daylight,
Dividing behind to the isolated fires that warm us.
Stone shore where the light breaks. A marble boulder, red
Veins in the white mist, smooth watery surface
Half sunk in grey sand, so hard and clear a thing that
We are put to guess what harm we could be in.

5
Shifting slow and vast extent viewed from the cliff
Top, so large as to raise questions talking
Of the whole of a life not just now and never to stop
Forgetting the recent deceits of resentment.
So calm and clear a thing as not to be around when
The earth is lost to those of mere power.

6
Closed earthlumps that collide together and fight
In the dark we seem, and the seeming harms us.
Yet we retain moments of casual success as we feed
The family in the caravan at a meal-time close to others',
Hid from the noisily munching ocean that
Thrusts behind my ear like a jewelled hat-pin.

7
Pyramids of light flickering on and off
On the sea surface, wedges of light, and us walking
Back to sleep on the abandoned table-top
Like the horizon's dinner. But instrument
Day and night for intercourse of love and pain.
The hills bend their heads to the hollow, homely hour.

8
Half crying sea birds above us in the night,
The constant breath of wind and the farmer's
Wife comes out with a little torch to feed
The geese. Baffled at yet another mother's
Triumph the sky stamps its foot and raises its hat
And charges out to sea rattling its tin.

II. SANDLOGGED

1

A double track, a furrow in the groundswell
From the house down to the sea, a corrugated breach
Between fields of sheep and wheat, down to the great sink.
Lined with hawthorn, bramble, blackthorn, bent
Gorse: Look how the wasps wallow in their graves,
Bathing in ripe blackberries, drinking their blood!

2

On either hand the seething fields and the full sea
Like life and death (though which is which)
And stark on the margin between them crowds
Of people, blurring over the sands like brush-
strokes, shouting and lying. You'd never believe
The cadences, the successions of fall.

3

Fields of wheat and pasturage halting at the level
Sea, where the fish shoals move in and out of reach.
And the beach crowd fills the bay with truce flags, pink
Blue and yellow, choral energy, manes iridescent
In the sunlight. And voices over the crashing waves,
Calling us out to face our enemies, gods of food.

4

Beyond the pleasure zone the cormorants skim steadily
Over their door to success crying at a pitch
Of failure (this is the solitary walk between crowds
On the clifftop pastures) and those crazy birds rush
To and from their island capital, unable to deceive
Themselves out of constant pleasure, constant thrall.

5

Souls of the crowd chorusing like a bell
Of a clifftop church, clear over grass and rocks, each
To each extolling what we have and like to think
Even despair is a shrewdness, a gesture meant
To spread the load. But, *das einsam,* ah, he craves
Gem-like contraries in the wrack, eyes in the dark hood.

6

Cooling and getting hungry we slowly
Walk back along the long sands carrying beach-
balls, blankets, fish-nets, binoculars, crabs,
Two small girls, books, towels, pebbles to keep, brush
And comb, bucket and spade; we carry what we conceive,
We carry carrying, being carried, fear and fatigue, we carry it all.

7

'I was ill, I couldn't sleep, I couldn't tell
What I was doing, so I came to this remote stretch
Of coast to fight the falsest persons I could think...'
And the sea this evening calm, a seething tent
Of blue-grey down smeared salmon and thick with caves.
Duplicitous, occultly tumultuous, screen of blood.

8

Almost asleep in the thin walls, undeliberately
I send my soul out like a night bird or a witch
To fly over the dark roads now silent of cars
And kids, skimming over the fields and black bushes
Over the white line that the wild waves weave
To settle on the headland, with your moon I fall.

III. SAILING, SAILING AWAY

1

Cold and wet, shout out the morning news:
No unit of life's pain will be eased this day
Or by being out here. The wind and the rain
Comb the field grass and units of time past
Rattle in our heads like pellets. Then space
Partitions and new warm promises crackle in our beaks.

2

Hell's Mouth. We scuttle across it in pairs.
We are traders: offerers, losers, those who
Claim to be givers are the worst of all.
Vast arc of shore where the sea never stops
Pounding the sand, days nights and years away.
Drear infinity. We cluster back to the car and lunch.

3

Next we stride across acres of jagged wet rocks and bruise
Insteps through the rubber. We get across the bay
Limping from shelf to shelf. There are departments of pain,
I suppose, and stores and garages. Our memories are massed
Against us but we slip them by in the trusty face
Of the arched instant. The car engine sputters into ticks.

4

Up and down the small valley the slow soft airs
Come to and fro, the stream purls and slips through
Old manganese workings: here and there a ruined wall,
Black holes in the valley sides. A stone dropped drops
Through nothing to distant water. And remember, far away
From here management decides hurt. Thank you, Mr Punch.

5

Why do we roam the land as if finding and lose
Everyone's time? There is nothing, but a grey
Gravel, a lost horizon, and a winding rain.
The slightest construct of care would cast
It all behind us like salt as we turn to face
A clearing sky to landward and a truly human fix.

6

Out on the open sea in a small boat there's
Suddenly nothing that isn't obviously true.
The sea top is a shining cloth. A dying gull
Sits in it like an old man in an armchair, props
A wing on the meniscus and joins the lift and sway,
Slowly giving himself to the one truth for ever head first.

7

The boat glides up the cove and grates on the loose
Stones. We mount the side cliff and wind up the day
In wet shoes with fishscales in our hair. The fisherman
Winds the boat up the shore, grinding slowly past
Heaps of marine detritus and wrack, to a safe place.
The light is almost gone. The sky curtain stirs and leaks.

8

Lying dozing late in the dark caravan, slight glares
Of lighthouse in a square on the ceiling every few
Moments, I send my consciousness out like a gull
Over the sea, away from the wasteful and gaudy shops
Of this life, away from my own tricks, indeed away
From the untruthful land. This dark divided church.

IV. FORTH OUT AND FIRST BACK

1

Driving up the coast road alone, a strange sense
Of being already dead, suspended where I pass
Over hills and through villages, incapable of harm
Or good to the people. My wish is neutral of course,
Provisional good sincerely upon unknown heads.
At a bad cliff corner the family leaps in my throat.

2

And on up the side of North Wales to a town
Selling death back to the lost people from industry
As coloured wrap with glims of distance, toffee stick,
And here-we-are-before-we-were-again (pastoral) that slides
Off before you can suck it. So buy quick and go,
On by the cool straits, the calm woods, and railways.

3

A country is no one's playground, no one's absence.
The mountains gather towards the sea, touched with thin grass,
And the coastal strip sweeps under in a curling arm.
A country must be sure to be more than a pause
In a life or a year. Pecking at the scattered threads
Of a remote history, small salt crystals stick to my coat.

4

The car park at Bethesda is roof height on the first crown
Of the valley side. I get out of the car and am instantly
In a large arena of lost industry, black scarp, headline nick:
Broken backed mountains and the sky stock full of clouds slides
Constantly over. Fears and promises flicker across us
Like shadow angels. We cleave between. Oh razor-sharp days!

5

Returning shortly to the car park at Bethesda the tense
Distance of farms and cottage rows on high shelves
Of the slate mountain, hit by the late sun, calm
And empty one senses an enemy. There is a torse
In the pastoral disc, an incision at the quarry beds
Letting through the dark. The day's width offers a groat.

6

There is an exit, a return. The road leads down
Into the valley, up and over this shifting, sliding geography
The car shoots past chapels and fortresses as quick
As a thought about where the enemy bides,
The false person I wanted to have a go
At. Cloven hillsides and the gulls flying sideways.

7

Nothing but evasion. I am in the men's
At Tudweilog, a tourist pub, thinking alas
I cannot define the root of harm without alarm
But I'm glad we sit together at the tables among gorse
Bushes children's swings and flower beds.
Brave harmony, from heaven's blast remote.

8

I squeeze my eyes and I'll blow your house down
Says the wind banging all night with blustery
Threat the tin panels of the caravan I'll kick
It to bits says the wind and life it rocks from side
To side and my mind is miles away in the still slow
Garden at the roots of the wind the voicing maze.

V. PERFORMING DOGS

1

Triangular field, pointing out to sea
Like an open beak, grass crown, feathery cliffs
Grazed thin, scattered with white flecks:
Feathers, wool, thistledown; I walk you this morning
End to end wondering how a new day won't reach more
Than an inch or two forwards or raise its head above shame.

2

So hive off on an excuse. Green road, hilltop ruins.
The solitary on the top track, fearful of farm dogs,
Pauses before the uninhabited, holiday cottage.
The wind is everywhere, the house another family's
Mindstock: childhood coin and wedding gift and
Promised past. Curtains closed. God save us from death.

3

And the great shore empty as far as you can see
Curving away, the waves grinding the quarried cliffs
Roaring into shingle, difficult walking, slow steps
Across the wind. Which if it led or were pointing
Anywhere would be a happy place, if the stones bore
Down the chute and rattled into boats under a trade name.

4

At Nefyn the travelling circus chimes and spins
The same old tale with its ropes and its dogs
As any other twisting mirror: that age in age
Out we detest what we become, and were, we hiss
And bark in the big pointed tent, we can't stand
Our ends and gladly hoot a fearsome breath.

5

God save us from half-life, it is also necessary
To note, sitting on the rocks eating fish and chips
At twilight, on the edge of the great curve, six
Mile bay watching people zooming and spinning
And riding the meniscus to what point or
Purpose we don't know but working all the same.

6

To their renown, for each is a space that wins
Its own centre, to which you and I are just dogs
Perhaps, just a circus game on the far edge
Of visibility. And some spin quietly and miss
Reward, but turn an acre of inhospitable land
Into a terraced garden, richly flawed, flowered, brief.

7

Love is where centres meet, I think I see,
Gathering mushrooms at twilight on the high cliff
Pastures, those white domes glowing like clocks
Here and there on the dark ground and the dawning
Sea light over my shoulder and they don't just grow or
Gravitate. But beam and echo name to name.

8

Lying awake at night my focus climbs
To the caravan skylight, barking dogs
At the farm, slowly, like old age
Mounting into a mortgaged tower, to kiss
The ghost of distance behind a shadow hand
And watch the sea, and stick there, weathered leaf.

VI. EATEN ZERO

1

Sometimes pasts are satisfied. It's like
Sitting on a café terrace over the deserted shore
In the evening sunlight sipping coffee in the thin
Savoury smoke of a barbecue as the waves reach
And reach in white fuss the great length
Of brown sands, where no claims reside.

2

The man who runs the beach shop and café at Porth Or
Decided one year to stay open in the evenings
And run a barbecue. No one came but it was
A gentle evening of deep sun and enough wind
From the sea to ruffle one's hair and move
An empty cardboard plate across the table.

3

It was a quiet summer, the concrete track
Bending down the fields to the pale shore
With no cars parked, no shouting, no one in
Sight but me and the man tending his beach
Barbecue which no one wanted and at length
Sitting motionless staring at the incoming tide.

4

No sound but the beating of waves and the generator
Engine behind the shop chugging away, things
Of residual time worn lightly because
A long past means a sure future and twinned
To the extent beside us is a sense of love
Where centres meet and agree to become unstable.

5

And the Centre of Anything is a Hell of Lack
The Mouth of Which is a Wide Shore
Feeding Generosity into a Rubbish Bin
Called EAT ME: a Country where Each
Has his Own Centre and Swells there in the Strength
Of Winning, a Hole as Deep as it is Wide.

6

These Spenserian periods passed before
My mind as I sat there thinking things
I cannot now recall and through my binoculars
Distinctly saw my father in a large winged
Armchair floating on the sea about half
A mile out, heading north and singing Handel,

7

'Gentle Morpheus, son of Night…' so like
A winged deity crossing the sun's red core
As it descends to the sea our senses move in
Traverse to the world's pull, that downy peach
That gets us in the end, and surely a strength
Of purpose survives the lapse of will, a sleeper's guide

8

Across the drowsy shore where centuries before
Hundreds landed daily, peasants merchants kings
Barefooted and lost, ghosting the outer rose.
The man in the white coat went and turned
The engine off behind the shop. The lamp above
My head flickered in the wind like a palmer's candle.

VII. EIGHT SEASIDE CHAPELS

1   *St Beuno's at Pistyll*

A place where people can shelter from one dream
In another, the finished dream, the walls hung
With medicinal herbs, the light dim and opaque.
Here you could silence the press and begin to address
Directly the separation of desires. Through thick
Stone walls the fruit trees rattle like the sea.

2   *Llangwnnadl*

Where travellers rest. I sit in the silence,
Doing and thinking nothing for as long
As I can bear it. Triple aisled light in which
I lose my name. But my stomach hurts, my nose
Bleeds, isn't that enough self for today or
Anyone? The lark turns, rest your shadow and belief.

3   *St Merin's Church*

Grassy humps in a clifftop field. A sunset beam
From the sea spreads through the stalks, among
Nettles and cow-parsley faint turf lines, dim shape
Of nave and apse. Here I lay my self crest
To rest, I hope, and crowned commoner O quick-
ly, turn north, where distance makes us three.

4   *Bryn Celli Ddu*

Gentle Orpheus, son of light. You are the sense
At the centre, the mechanism through which the long
Beam passes at morning and evening, the bridge
Across the heart in the darkness that grows
Daily finer as the body ages and at the core
Of which a line of light writes final relief.

5 *Llandudwen*

What is that relief? O wait and see, the cream
Of liberty is not to know, the prize is the sung
Response echoing in a stone room the shape
Of a person built over a grave. Cornered. So dress
Your anxious head proudly in the thick
Brightness. Be that engine which learns to be.

6 *Capel Anelog*

And this site of which nothing at all remains
Was where the final question was asked on the long
Pilgrimage to Bardsey. 'Did you remember to bring
The tin-opener?' or 'Did you really expect the rose
To be an inner answer to unwelcome law, or,
If now is almost time isn't it far too brief?'

7 *Ffynnon Fair*

Now is over, over the hill. The waves scream,
The waves crash. Here on the brown rocks hung
Over nothing, here at the impossible landing, cape
And hood gathered close, distance is set to our best
Sight – for we saw people prepared to stick
To their truth. The island lies before us on the sea.

8

The salt raging within, the ravenous remains
Of the earth running in the vein, reaching the tongue
And bursting into courtesy. An everyday thing,
Far removed from the sickness and errors that bring
Every day of self to a weary and troubled repose.
Far away on the night shore the salt wings close.

VIII. SEAWATCH

1

Sunk in a grass hollow in the cliff, my station,
A grave green chair. The sea is blue green white,
The sea is grey and folds, the sun is split
And the clouds are a fire. Truth is never
Quite the same, its quantum cracks but
Like a three quarter moon hands down adoring stead.

2

Which is a pulsing certitude a gently
Wavering assurance. The sea throws
Silver coins at the rock. The whimbrel, that shuns
The sight of man, passes down the coast
And a heron follows, for if we are still
We are welcomed, if we are one we are met.

3

A wind up the coast, scent of a milling nation
Traverses the brow so calm a bright
Disposal is for a moment carved a bit
Above his hand and for a fraction the ever
Fractious lark curves over his head. He says I am but
A shepherd of the plain, without ambition, later dead.

4

Stuck in the middle of life, that ungently
Grinds of ruin while the sea is a knife thrown
Across the earth. This evening it darkens
From grey to white and draws at what cost
I don't know the light from the fields until
Swathed in shade I let it go for sixpence net.

5
My O my I thought I had a notion
To validate with truth this brittle
Spending, at every smile and every bite bent
Closer to the ground shifting the weather
Onto my back and wearing like Canute
A crown of clifftop grass and soil all the way to bed.

6
Now it is the middle of night. The empty
Waves continue to knock on the land, down
There. Still some light clings to the sea and the floss
Flickers on the rocks. Human will bearing its star-crossed
Ensign haunts the black interior for good or ill. Spots
Of rain on my coat, are you with me yet?

7
And it will be good. The clouds open: a true equation
Dominates the eastern sky, bright Queen of it:
The shadow of the earth rises across the firmament,
Proving us truly here. And working hard, wherever
Some portion of true hope lies open in the cut
Of a single life (knife, wife, strife, head).

8
When I get back to the caravan it is twenty
To four. Stumbling in the darkness I hear a moan
Of blame, a sleeping urge to die and quit this mess.
But there is no speed at all, no wily ghost.
I tuck the blankets round me heavy with dew,
Closing on sea moon and all, but alive in you.

Sea Watch Elegies

The world-sheet breaks time open
We are the waste some of which gets called back
Curved back to surround random events like
A shell and offer the future a site
A line that stands a long stone
Against the star a trust that opens
At its point – we are set again we are
Daily beings, yearly ideas, we stick.
The silver turmoil warns and arms us,
Passing home.

Δ

Cloud-sheet lit from below
Orange bands
Wind in grass
A man walking on the cliff
Passing measures
Serrated perspectives
Accumulated lives
Replaced persons
Measured thoughts
Choired land.

Δ

Like a night-watchman over the sea
A shepherd of the plain, not without ambition, I
Stay, still enough for the balance to rest its
Question here.

Cirque of rain clouds to the west
A wet moth clinging to a grass stalk
Questioning welcome

Dark grey, turbulent sea, flecked waste,
Quick moving air on the cheek
Hater of governments, lover of order

World order – Answer it, this
Mindless power. There is nothing to stop us
Loving in peace and constancy.

To end up alone in a grey house
Grim grey seaside bungalow
A few gathered belongings
Persisting with a work
Of uncertain provenance or future
Dark wine in the evening
A collection of tapes
Without you I am nothing,
A leaf in the wind an old fox
Walking unhurriedly to earth.

Δ

Black rags cast in the
Grey sky, light infused
With meaning
Meaning take your stick and go
Everything is busy without you
And so he does
To a room, and lights a lamp.
Wave noises through the walls
Black scraps cast on a page
Defying passage

Δ

Alone in the house
A green shelf over the sea
The few things needed
Work to be done
Certain and necessary
Dark wine in the evening
Various musics
Always with you
Wherever you are
Set on earth.

Waves (dim things) pushing at the land
All night through the thick walls
Begging, thoughtless begging
Suddenly stops and we agree
We agree to live in a world
To live in a world
That does have worldness.

Δ

'As he lived so he died,
In mild and quiet sort'

Like a night watchman or a
Welsh farmer steadily

Binding the fences
Calming the afflicted

And his belief
In worldness

Leaving me alone or worldless
Up here on the cliff top at night
Everyone asleep behind me
Stop pushing, roll over.

Δ

Two hundred and forty-fifth wave
Rolls over, two hundred and forty-sixth
Everyone busy elsewhere I
Watch nothing on purpose
And worth every second too, as the vast
Haul of dark earths our core.

Δ

Night winds hugging the coast
And night birds sailing
Over the ground-light, over the sea.

One lit window, over there, along the cliffs
Attending day. Let me
Too be nothing but

Δ

And never stop,
Lay the pale stones together
On the edge of the land
That warn the traffic and
Shepherd the stray
Thoughts to their purpose.
Set aside a tenth of the profit
For the commonalty.

And at last, pale streaks across the sky
Thin cloud televising dawn
Ice crystals
Float over the house
And black shed.

Δ

The grass again.

Δ

Always saying more
There is no more to say
But to beg release and
Order it down: world go
Under, go under world.
For we hate it. We've
Had enough. Enough world
Enough wine. Enough cold/hope.

Δ

And creep into bed at last
Into darkness in the day
And peace and closure in the plains of loss.
And the pains of lessness fall.

Between Harbours

1

Long and tiring journey
through car zones

Arrive 'washed out'
back of neck, eyelids, shoulders

Walk down to the sea, where
metal stays sheathed.

All the stones are rounded
and form sentences together it

Doesn't matter what you hate and drink it
matters what the heart answers dying dying.

2

It matters when, the heart questions,
dying to finalise these taunting distances

And be where you live. A wild home
or a protecting distance, where

The stones beat against the sea
growling and grinding together to form

A musical sentience, darkening as the
earth turns and the gulls descend.

Wine, supper, silence and sleep. The stones say
every breath is kept safe to the end.

3

In the little cove the stones rattle and squeak,
a thin stream comes down to the sea and the
slight waves tonight tap idly on the rocks.

My night camera, favourite spot, journey's end.
Between driven earth and halting sea
the tide like a little washerwoman scrubs

The pebbles smooth and grades them in strata
and with Beckettian astringency repeats
what little she knows every eight seconds.

Further out the real sea, a vast self a vast unit
that pulls away from time and sorrow and knows
only its own sense, and picks at the shore

As at the edges of an itchy scab. Its own hero,
its own journey its own faint curiosity at
otherness and love. I walk back up the cove

To the fence that separates all this from
the possible, and traverse it at a 5-barred gate,
waking the farm dogs. I head for the small

Window-light across a vast indigo haze
belonging only to the world, pebbles
in my pockets, arguing about the waste of days.

4

The sea seems to breathe slowly, and to fall
one step at a time, because the universe

Is what it is, calling and calling and calling,
attracting everything to its path, death.

A red mullet falls out of it and I
slit it with a sharp knife avoiding

The poisonous spikes, setting aside
the blue liver and shiny bowels.

I make rather a mess of it, failing to clear
the smallest bones, but it makes a good meal

Eaten with care, with world trust
under the conflicting messages

5

A few minutes on the shore, in the small cove
the body complaining as the stones roll

And shift underfoot and the substance
of the sea changes, becoming infected.

Lies told proudly by the Thames change the sound
the sea makes on a small Welsh shore

More than they change the welcome behind
the lit window. Somewhat more than the earth,

Some priority, cuts the haze and paves
the difficult ground the failing

Body tracks to the end. Head wobbling
on top of it saying I've lost my watch.

6

A figure standing on the little shore like a statue
a post sunk into the shingle as night slowly falls
the noise of breaking fills the air and little

Wave rims ply around his shoes. All the white lines
and pale fences of dark England snaking through
his body as he stands there like a notice board

At the water's edge, all the roads and service stations
of his way there abseiling down his digestive system
like the belly-dance down a Cimabue crucifix from panel

To panel to the end, the foot, the fixed point on which
the horizon spins into reverse and the midnight special
shines its ever-loving light on me.

7

The length of anyone's life, a gathering of traces,
dim ghosts on the dark surface of memory swaying
from side to side like a boat coming quietly to harbour
crunching on the stones and stopping.

To bring back what is gained, to climb the steep
track up the cove the sea growling below and the wind
combing my hair I smile back and head for
something less permanent, and much more clear.

Back the twisty path up the cliff to the headland,
and cross the dim field towards a known condition
and a short time, that sees a long way and is
over before you know it, I can't wait.

To deny eternity and lie under blankets between
thin walls while the gas cylinder growls and
asked the question answer Yes: this brevity,
and separation, is what I came here for.

8

Red gas-fire glow, dark space, blankets firm on
cheek and shoulder, slight wind noise outside

And that thing standing down there on the shore
like a life-belt holder, scratched and marked

With the colours of earth, full of
twisting cloud and longing for peace.

By the water's edge where probably the first life
on earth floated idly towards the stones

Or gods and goddesses from the curvature of the earth
rode to shore in a wooden boat called Absolute Certainty

And met a notice saying Welcome. No Parking. Pay
at the kiosk. And saw a waterfall twisting down the cliff

An old man warming his hands at an electric fire
and a list of indulgences pinned to a door, which opened

And I woke up in earth's brightness. Smoke
rising from the harbour, wet grass, hunger.

III

OSPITA

Wirksworth to Cambridge, 1983–1987

1.
Seeking a bearing point on hurt I find
Hollows and rooms in the thick of the night,
A building hard at work flashing its bright
Offers into the star dome. Consigned
Forward I bring my name in a sealed jar
To the steps up, pay the slight fee, assent
To slow harm by the covering letter.
Entering into purpose distance springs
Back from the horizon to hold the cup
The bitter cup but true, of flesh-driven earth
(This night is the day outside the dream, this
Tableau my government, or family wish)
And deep in the brickwork think of asters
Blazing on the far links in slow birth.

2.
I bear my coat and cast to a senior,
A new-old faithfull, who should know the coils
And corridors of the heart, the slender
Ghost smiling to the third tune. What is false
Be set into a pestle, what rings be
Represented as an inner garden
Open to Sirius, one and the same be
Ground and broiled and spoken as your answer.
The house is quiet, old radio music
In the walls, scissors on the table, streaks
Of blood in the sink. A call in the night,
I get up, white coat, glance out at the rain
On the glass, attend. What do I exchange for pain?
Holding a stranger's thin arm I turn down the light.

3.
Calcium night light. Suddenly a man
Shouts, 'Orpheus!' and the dying die,
The sick sleep on, the deserted bitterly cry
And I count the call as best I can across
The fogs of routine silence; word that holds
The earth into a chiming whole, enfolds
Love in a capsule coated with loss, never
Cedes to wishful death but calls us to drop
Our trades and be again that whirring top
On the mountain ridge, screaming down river a pain
Of incompletion, fall medallion, cut
The human heart to song. And it will, don't
Turn the light out, see to the day's wounds, won't
Stop our good hands tying, that sweet moan again.

4.
A man shouts in pain, the voice constructs
A door. The god batters his forehead
On our simple attendance, the fruit
Of centuries' observance. But to eluct
Wisdom from hurt – any hospital bed
Would burst into flame at the mere thought.
The music coils within: a long solo,
And the final voice squeezed from a lump
Of flesh held over a sink said and we tried
Our best to stifle that singing, 'Do
What you will to ease me over the hump
Of death I belong to the great outside.
My burning lust courses at last through Hell.
The pain of what I couldn't manage spreads like a bell.'

Passing Measures

5.
This house constructed as an escape
From harm is unlikely to escape
Its own folly as a new escape
From meaning and source of new dolour.
A woman shouts down a corridor
A real name: 'Sidney! Sidney! Sidney!'
A door slams bone shut. I am sorry
To have life shot through by her call
I can't dream any harder the fall
Of light onto the wet leaf, the stain
Of nurture on a simple erection.
In the end she is right: the rape
Of endless joy and everyone's to blame.
Out on the lake the long boats wane.

6.
At night the walls are blank but we can hear
The plovers crying in the dark fields, their
Wings beating over waves of wheat. Downstairs
Someone opens the piano and strikes a chord
That tenses the flanks of hope. Again there
Is a silence in which the lapwings graze
The ear tips and clouded underwing
Flashes across the sky. Then where and where
In this globe of health we balance and bear
From room to room, where is a lasting thing?
Where is a good done that also stays it?
Someone attempts the new soft swing but out
In the earthglow between mind and chest
Brilliant metallic birds like kisses dive to rest.

7.

The man dies and the bell sounds across
Grass and sea and mixes with the gulls.
The dream sleeps into the morning, turns
On its side and drifts down the coast
Under the grey cliffs and buildings
Dedicated to healing but now
Empty and dark at dawn, the sharp keens
Of the white hens warning us to be slow.
We comfort as if there were no cost,
As if pain could be stilled to patience
Separately, and the story lost.
Good men have died lost in empty time
But loading their bite on th'intrinsic nation
Steady as grade of light, or yellow chime.

8.

Time drags its heals on the dreamer who hears
His body calling him like a discant
Semaphore, a sign hung on a fruit shop
Under the castle wall. The sheets are bright
Anger the oxide of faith and he fears
The fall into humanity, the slant
Of honey and cream; those fair lids droop
And he is solitary on the white
Road across the heath, he is close to tears
For the imperfected lives he couldn't want
To bring to their moment of concord and float
On further life. The swallows are in flight
Over the russet fields crackling with fear
As he enters the day's gate as is right.

9.

They draw his body from the centre out,
A decisive goodness. He lies flat out
On the shore counting ills. The waves enter
His total wealth into books of sand.
It's enough. They are happy to inter
His soul in lime and ash for the sake
Of a comfortable end, the winter
Of our success rebound in angel cake
But winter is true numbers that blister
From the corpse in a field, alternating
Black and white name-tags that flitter
Like sarcens in the treetops. Small birds sing
His centre into holes in the snow and grey
Doctors weeping envy send him on his way.

10.

I walked out on the morning of May 12th
The blades were bright and coy and loud
Thick with languages I walked without stealth
The fields of angry farmers, proud
To be harmless and legal, half and half,
No one could fathom my strong shoes
There is no paradise but tongue of love.
I walked all day, I heard no news,
When twilight filled the air with gravities
I descended, heart full and slow
Down the dim fields dotted with stones and sheep
To the house in its bank of trees
The fire, the food, the Gurney piano,
Having my wonderful labour to keep.

IV

from NOON PROVINCE

Les Bassacs / Cambridge, 1986–1989

Arriving at Dawn

Valuable small acts. Arriving
To the standard breakfast,
Wanting an ordinary thing
That people believe in
Such as the day begins,
Keeps them on and together.

Dawn-worn,
A variety of travellers
Pile out of the train and shuffle into the cafeteria
And neglecting in first light
Pride of office, take their turns, asking
For the complete, the integral.

Market Day

How it fills the town to its purpose,
Stalls heaped with olives, cheeses,
Chickens and doves, fills the squares
With food and clothing, the streets with
Garlic and mushrooms, ordinary things
As we speak them, full of knowledge
And desire – crowds under plane trees,
Sound of talking all through the town,
Cavern of image the mouth keeps its
Tone, retains its modest expectation,
Pulses in tune to the pocket,
The ordinary day that earns it.
Wild lavender honey from the hills.

Roofwatch

1.
Day and night the sky arches over
Hills and plain turning against
The earth, clouds springing
From the dark wooded edge fan
Over the farmed land and at
Night the plethora of stars
Turns clear and sure and
Compact in their terraces
Above a veiled and separated ground
O fine in their farming the stars
Rally and exit all night.

2.
Full adoration without question.
The white rock breaks on the wooded slopes
Over there and the sun dies constantly
Over the vinefields, burning out fruit.

Repletion without any question
And no curriculum to the world
No credentials you would ever believe
For the sun burns cherries out of twigs

And the stars thresh mind pages
To a solitary and quiet wish
To line a space before we turn
To love's raging difference.

Meditations in the Fields

1.
Strolling in the olive groves and
Orchards, dry sky and hot stones, hard
Light and Ockeghem on the walkman –
I time the intervals. They are tightly numbered
And of such extent, such meeting parts
That all the time I wasted in disuse
(Bed, social time, infant fear)
And wasn't treading the mind's width
Is reckoned to my regret and returned
Untouched to the earth, or so it seems.

2.
Gazing at the ground
Wild thyme and sparse grass
The blue bellflower, Aphyllanthus
Monspeliensis, hanging over the stones
Between the cherry trees patches of sunlight
And Josquin in the earphone I
Am told out. We receive everything
And return it, in the flesh.
Now because it is charted. The flesh
Fruits so fulsome and glad precisely
As farmed, didn't they say?

3.
Pausing in the hot vine fields, Brumel
Through the wire seeming to say
That mutual enemies debate in the
Chambers of the heart, as Dante
Definitely said, and a small spirit
Pleads to the soul through a thin wire,
Regain your place. And sweet and low
(As thyme fills the air) O scouring focus
Neglect our substance if you will but
Shepherd this instant to its kingdom as only
The sharpened spirit kens and quickly –
Shew mercy on those good shepherd on

Us ourselves, the very ones who
Sit alone for their receipt in a foreign field,
Send us to our remembrance, it's time
Clear enough through the crackle and fuzz
Death's silence leading each tone
Onwards, to lock the door
And fall into human length.

4.
Anywhere in the world the
Mind wakes while I
Contemplate a field corner and now
Lassus in the speaker telling
Of a rose entrammelled in the years,
Surviving as so much else
Continues to exist, so much
Pain and disappointment
The rose we make again, that you would
Never recognise or credit as that same
Armonia, that unfolding, clad in
The regency of the moment –
A silent and remote
Fold in the edge of the hills
Where a few things grow and I
Harvest exclusive result.

Lines at the Pool above St.-Saturnin

Alpine swift (the white chested) carving the air
And a quick wind from the hills redolent of
Pine and lavender rides the rocky cleft
Skimming the surface our sight remains
Unpolitically tabulated / Innocent in delight
It is perfectly right, forswearing a life
Fixed in ratio to demand like a permanent
Insect-target for the flashing creature.
All we ask is that the heads of the town
Account justice faithfully.

What do we know of world and detail who can't
Compete with the swift for vantage in the
Dream of earth? That speed of gain and grace
Leaves us standing, lost in our weight and
Hesitance, lost in delight at the fruitless sight
Of the species pilot fixing history to a dive.

But delight closes and light rises. The limbs
Tremble and bow to the mind that pokes
The blazing episphere of day at its fault
Facing world torsion with what? with a politeness,
A reasonable plea: *Raste Krieger, Krieg ist aus.*
Beautiful silent answers move over the hills.

So among ruined walls and broken arches
We foreswear a hope that has no substance
Set sticks on bricks, gather truthful items from
The surrounding area and algebraize a sequence.

Later the lake dims, the birds retire
The mind or something silently similar
Hovers in plagal trust in the crumbling air;
Talking to death at the ancient gate
Where the locust pauses, and the woody stalk.

Escape from our Uncaring

Mid-day heat at the ochre-quarries,
We have pulled the earth aside and left
Ourselves without shadow, without
That dark doubt that saves us.

And stamp on in absolute certainty:
£8,000,000 for a Van Gogh.
('No cost is too high.')

Returning to the fields, the dark cherries
Are dying to be pulled. In the village
The new bread swells and cracks.

Lacoste

The landscape is a thought thing, it
Has been thought as a gift and as a burden.
We drive through someone's book to
The Marquis de Sade's castle, where misthought
Has left not a trace.

House prices flutter and electronic pastoral
Beats the air to no result: the true architecture
Speaks only *vulgare illustre,* heartstuff,
Dialect/reduction/vantage stand flat to the side,
Everything except justice is an impertinence.

It is a crowned structure, a hill
Rearing to intellect and lust as a burden
Patiently and proudly borne, set
Clear above the fruiting plain
Brighter stone than star because thought
                                    flawed

Recalling Lacoste

Back at night in an old room,
Total country silence. Dim bulb,
Moth at window, bread and cheese,
Côtes du Rhone Beaumes de Venise 1985
Cheap but delicately heartening.
Silent tonight, reading a pocket
Guide or Dante and thinking of home.

The castle ringed the summit in white, the village
Houses were its skirts trailing into the ridged fields.
One does what one does, of course, but only
What we know we do does much good.
The village dog barks twice and stops. Thin
Noise of someone's music. There is
A question always at hand, sometimes a horror,
Which we are entitled to neglect, with
Courtesy. And could do much
More but look at the time.

Counting the Cost (Syllables at Night)

We are back and silent, no
Fire tonight, dull light
Of the moony bulb, the door
Latched, the shutters to.

Count the silence: seven five
Count the silenced, oh
Millions, lost in the sky and
Scattered on the earth

Never to be spoken or
Known by any name
Whose continuity is
With us in the night

Night of other nights
When we were silent
And the earth turned ahead of
Our silent petrified thought.

Teaching us to be nothing
In distant foreign corners
The earth turns the dark
Into truth. Wait there.

Up the Big Hill and Back by Ten

Walking the mind, walking the prosody,
Uphill, hour upon hour on a stone track
Through the garrigue and straight up the hot hill.
It is numbered. The little oaks whisper
The numbers are there whatever you do
Or say, no rests or interludes, sheer calm
Continuing as the numbers last, when
The numbers are full you are there. No one
In. A bright green lizard on a stone.

So we turn, descend, count on. A wasps' nest
Up a tree, a mantis' egg-sac under
A stone. Unkempt mountain lavender fields
Thyme, alkanet, early purple orchid
Remote farms up in the hills where much more
Than entire lives have been played out and love
Has been doubled or quartered and time clicks.

Politics is a play of fear. Fearful
Clicking of time in the hills as if a
Life is never enough meaning. It is
More than enough. A book in my pocket
By Dante, a pocket edition. When
We get back we'll have bread and cheese with wine
And count the day to its figured close.

Resolution and Interdependence

We are together we are lost
In dazzling light in the limestone
Gullies and terraces of a complicated hill
In a blaze of flowering shrubs. Taking
Goat paths between drystone walls
Stooping under laden branches stepping
Among swallowtails we find our way
Together and what does it ever mean
But action and purpose, to be together?
A stupid simple thing to say as if
Destruction weren't also action and purpose
And being lost among flowers.
We must get back and think ourselves
Carefully apart and trade our love limb
For limb. As the swallowtails swarm.
As the dying flare.

Real Number

Reaching for food
Offered I disappear
Into a vetch stratum.
Stay with me, guilt
Is a square plot,
An abandoned garden
Or olive grove
In front of a chapel
With a locked door.
We say nobody seems
To mind. Soft wine
Raises our spirits to
The foliation band.
Whoever says he minds
Will be offered a glass.

Just a Song

Dark on the upper fields, the bushes
And small trees clumps of blackness
In a grey haze. The walker, alone, has
Slight but simple script to find his path,
Pale streaks on the ground. The moon en-
closes the air, the bullfrog creaks
In the silence, the grasses fidget and lapse.

He listens to the silence and hears
Nonsense, eyeless jokes in a dark hall.
His mind runs ahead of it becoming
Leader of a quiet procession
Trailing down the hillside between fields,
Holding the moon on the end of a stick

To see his way. The message is clear
And timely. His best intentions mesh
With the world's world and fall back towards
His interclusion and so they must
Or Death gets double six and an extra go,
Because the littleness of his world succeeds.
Look how he hangs from the moon!

The path leads clearly down to the edge
Of the slope and rejoins the road where
It hangs over the wide valley scattered
With house lights and a steady glow
From behind the far hills. Someone has left
An old white horse in a field with food
Water and shelter, standing through the night.

Stating the Case

Walking through the fields, not to create
Harm that devolves back to worlds.
A black cricket with orange knees, beaming
Yellow furze, a white butterfly with black
Edging and sage underwing. Listen

While I tell you. Blue iris newly unwrapped,
When you're nearer to death than birth
The coin begins to pass more openly
Like the earth at a good conjunction.
A five-pointed violet star.

Then the wheatfield bloody with poppies.
I think this swelling bright horizon
Holds us (passing) at our best yet
Since we don't know where final justice lives
And death isn't quite enough to meet the need

For it, we care desperately to create a good
Past us, taking to risk an edge of harm.
In a sudden hot hollow a mass of brown
Butterflies and round the corner an
Orange car containing.

The Telephone Box on the Edge of the Cornfield

Letters and numbers spray from our minds,
Settle on the wires in unbroken code. The car
Sees everything with two hollow eyes
Sees there is nothing to see but signs
At choices. This is what our minds
Are reduced to, living in this world.

So we get out and stand by the field leaning
On the box and light breezes play the
Corn like Mbira. There is red and slight
Blue undertext, disclosed where least
Expected from time to time.

And the heart is said to be a
Rare blue object in a red matrix
Surrounded by the yellow goods.
Consuming and lashing strokes. On the
Border of which a mind or surface
Pauses, keeping all this together.

Last Night

(1)

Stretched in the stone chamber
Awake and listening
To the dark stone silence that
Grew from nothing. Final justice
Lives in our hearts.

And nothing here is ours, we came
And went like a night moth, a few
Tourists were here for a week
They stayed up late in thought by
The single lamp.

Exactly so, exactly us
Fishing for quick messages
In the wind along the wall,
Histories of earth that signal
To the whole heart

That the world is there out there
In the dark full of hope and
Silence and calling to a
Centre. A single bell rings
Across the valley.

Slowly the heart unfolds, slowly
The mind weighs. Ordinary events
That hold people together and
On into day and year in
Spite of loss.

Helpful and obedient too,
Passing faithful to the
Substance that writes itself
Across the night and back to our
Lives in the end

(2)

Sensing a power that
Answers death I move to the
Window and nothing happens.
'A beautiful and gentle wild thing
Pierces my breast'

And turns there and chambers and
Libraries fan out from that
Simple point and a music
Farms the air. How it
Bells the close!

And we are cast against
Injustice in wild longing,
Screw our eyes at the world which
Won't settle into peace until
It is far too late it is over.

There is nothing but darkness out there
And something flies out, some creature
Of breath, over the hill calling
And calling like to like
One power to one life

As if a person could do a thing
But inhabit a language that makes sense
Whose periods follow themselves in
Tune to distance and arrive
Ahead of harm.

Something in the dark quiet
Night whispers in my head after
Tearing my breast and tells me look there is
Nothing there, there is no
Rose but truth unfolding

(3)

Light and substance. We are caught
In a tangle of seeking
Consequence. And the winner
Weeps at his success, to have taken on
Earth's thankless gain.

Refuse it. Act on the very
Minim of reluctance and the city
Rears behind the hill –
Calm terraces, theatre
Of entire lives where flesh

Unfolding turns at last
To shore, to earth's arc, bright
Moon on the tree jagged edge of the
Black hill out there for a moment
Which is a moment

Of complete certainty never to be
Relinquished; heart infoliate the only
Lasting or wanted thing.
And the stream running under the wall
And the paling ash

We leave behind, shoulder
Luggage and are forgotten.
Leaving an empty house, the night
Bird perched on the roof ridge
Pealing death out

Of hiding, out of the horizon.
Then a slight paling begins, night
Turns and trots down the valley, dreams
Wrapped in darkness and world
Break into day.

Orange to Chartres

Stay and work, stay and work,
Build machines in the garden.
The leaf opens to show a chrysalis,
A tortoise suddenly crosses the path.
Oh stay anyway, work to the planet's
Demand: how to pan that mothering arc
Away from worlds to here, and come
To know at some impossible distance
How love comes finally to a start.

A model of the heart, standing
Across the river. It shines at night,
Covered in creations and justices.
Opercular: a closed work, that stands
There like an old man in the sun –
A message of arcaded days, shadowed access
To what we are. And can and will.
Loved justly because a credit succeeds us.
At which the star leaps into the rose.

Slow Meditation in the Café-Bar Les Caves du Mont Anis, Le Puy

Sometimes a feeling comes on me saying that to love the very savour
of human being is such a rare thing, to love a kind of savour or centre
of what we are, which is an ordinary thing but the only truth we wholly
know, the only fullness without interference, our own stake in time:
the person being here. That is not a sudden or dramatic thing, that
does not imply wide revelation, but is here all the time. And on rare
occasions we notice, that there is a truth at our pivot, that it fans out
through us, that we can act and speak on its tide.

And it is never quite singular, you know, never quite alone, however
much we shirk the focus there is always that telling chime; to sit alone
in a cave under the cathedral is to smile at a library of honesty. And
welcome what we can of it. We can hardly move without that prime
informer the tongue across time and worlds funnelled down onto
what we perceive and learn. We cannot even guess at the weight and
pressure of true souls informing a slight movement of the lower lip,
a faint stirring at the back of the head moving towards language, a
feeling as of the slow dropping of veils, the narrowing of world light
to an entrance.

This feeling says very little, it says only that the light is not yet out and
every point in the world continues to exist as every person who ever
did exist had a centre which transmitted itself into a vocabulary and
on into hope. Even those, I think, who preferred hurt. But it is a feeling
which occurs in a pause and protected from both sides, protected and
fuelled by the days and futures of searching, obedient, action.

Passing Measures

Protected from what anybody ever did by what they might. We cannot arrange for such pauses.

It says a little more too, in a kind of weariness inhabiting the resilience and ease of the feeling, almost an edge of anger to the blissful prescience like a line of shadow marking the edge of an arch. It mentions that we also hate this life and all its distracting obstacles. It says that the angels, in the tympanum, with their serrated wings, are more beautiful and more human than the dark twisted flesh of our comedians and newscasters because they also assure us that we are also not here, also not anywhere on this striven planet at all, we have already come to an end and a line and a syllable mark out the wonderful pleasure of not having to be where we are put, not having to be here in this lying cave. One window opening onto a stone wall. That is to say, this is not a mixed feeling, but a feeling with an edge.

This block of sense is beyond harm while it stays. Its tranquil inwardness offers goodness indirectly, as the world understands, shadowed in honour and fidelity, starting with those we know best. For it exhorts us to declare ourselves in full. And at an enjoining of calm by which the offer must be repeated until it is taken, falling again and again to lay the coin at your feet, to make verses. Craftily glossing the past into trust via forgetting it rather precariously opens the future through its own delicately poised moment and totally assures the hesitant bearer: *the end is in sight,* minutely, so slight it almost hurts to locate. And what is your secret then in the years to come of elsewhere and departure, what does it matter then to have gained a self rise? It is returned anyway, the earth wants it all back. Stay with what you are. Work the burden and blind fear out of continuance by no more than a noticed edge, a flicker of grass, a simple attendance – that is, to shepherd this moment to its kingdom, as we have slowly learned in centuries of script. The continuance held in the instant and helpless out of it, like a lost child. And that is to say, I know nothing but this table. On which is represented by curious skill, a pattern of welfare. A pattern of warfare. A map of faring.

V

SELECTED POEMS 1966–1996

Urizon

I am from language and will return to language
        and no one will know
              what else I might have been

Storm waves blot out the lights
along the sea-front of Hove and Brighton
not the back-streets of Manchester or
networks of estate roads south of
Stockport I was never there;
the same wind curves across the land
tearing thick grass on the
Derbyshire moors where
                   I've never been.
And the centre of all this tumult,
calm centre of this raging absence
a plastic substance woven into
the rocks and meteorology
of the continental shelf
a morphosis the colour of blood
and winter sunsets, out of
dreams of limestone, coagulates
                  into
a device capable of speech
and silence, that can
turn the world on a syllable,
for good or ill.

A Column of Air

The wind across the chimney top
   vibrates a column of air and a low drone
 fills the room. I think the waves
     are tearing at my chest
   I think the stormwind has my mind
   petrified with its monotonous message from the sky
Keep me warm and hold me intact
       in this rout
 pillow my head away from that monody
   the stars are little sucking mouths
     all over the sky
  they draw my soul out of the house
 into the weather, set to their
  awful tune, the air
    rushes over, they pulse
     with pain at the extremes of cold and heat
       where it is one thing / a white
 condition where men of earth cannot breathe
   the ground pushed away under my feet
     the comfortable earth /
 a molecule of water
     charges in from the sea
 curves round the house and heads off inland at speed
   hold me to the floor before I cast off
     the rest of my atoms to follow those
   the wind has already sloughed off my face
    and posted to the distant hills
  my arm out: have me here
    bed me in my
   fear of the dead men in the sky

     Because I have learnt their names
     and they don't like it.

Valley of the Moon

Walking the night valley
under the moon, all the flowers
hidden away all the colours
departed, the colourless wind
falls on the grey slopes, the stream
crashes down the rockface

There is something in us not in the least
concerned for any present want
but working only and constantly against
the shipwreck of an entire life

There is an elegance in it, a music
continual, relentless as if
it need never stop and then
smiling turns to its close, under
no constraint

This is the valley, the true one
very difficult and at night
full of strength

from *The Linear Journal*: four poems

(1)

And it *is* true, that we move across
a whole range of intellectual/erotic paradises
Monday, Tuesday, etc.

'I feel an immense calm in your presence'
or 'Your presence fills me with a desperate agitation'

The day is calm, a variety of sea,
the traders waiting for weeks and weeks
in the imaginary harbour
or a slow train across the reddish plains
for days, specks of fire on the far mountains at night

ending in
a summer palace, fantastic traceries
in white stone, the light is inside it
and gardens with fountains and dwarf cedars
we say we 'want' that, meaning
it is there, we have heard of such a thing.

We bear it in mind, for hours sometimes,
imprecisely, in corridors and offices
that delicate act of transfer keeps us on,
holding out against
further violence of this kind,
the harm it does our
proper knowledge of heat
that we have
in the days we move across, the spectrum
held among us.

(2)

I feel terrible. I feel like
the bearded fungus on this conifer
and in this rotting state I suddenly sense
immediate victory, no

ironies attached; it doesn't matter
how I feel, ever. I'm through
permanently with immediacy and victory and
being-born and

feeling-around / acres of rich colour
run off from my eyes into the luxuriant distances
where two shepherds are calling to each other
the songs of yes and no

and how can so much warm air
draw itself so loosely through the blue-green crystal
what does it want, shaking the strands and banners of decay
or petrify someone's heartaches into amber globules?

Shepherds are calling translucent cries
in the shattered and untrustworthy distances
from which the wind is due to turn
cold any minute now, from its source

through almost infinite gradations of density
we stand and swivel, continents
apart, defiantly ignoring
the whole crust in beckoning array.

(3)

And what do we love anyway (here I am coming up to
a mountain) and would it be some kind of vortex
that slowly approaches holding out its hand
across the Persian carpet

          like a wolf's tooth out of the woodlands

which means what are we doing? what is it that keeps us at it? is it
the note that with all the terrible alterations the hot and cold
and in and out and however much more-or-less at the mercy at a
loss at the end of the tether we still have a marked declination
a pulse in the roadline, a vocation towards purpose and probably
capable, of. Or quite simply
you do not become a merchant of harm
because   obviously

(stroking the hairy quarters
of some dog, passive on the lawn, who could have known
or warned anyone what the extension of love involved?
that it cannot be had for a song
or a quick distraction in the colours but constant grind
incapable of holiday whatsoever because no one is going
to complete the self in this field where too much

is to be had at too postponed an offer, set forward and
elsewhere, hammered down on the loss borne by those people
not seen or thought of, which the music is raising and
drawing closer – at every minute a song is minted
much higher than promise, and in this hope
I ventured once, groping in the dark, and burnt my hands
on the most amazing things.

(4)

After which to fall howling into life step by step
the secret risks under every stone we have come thus far
and you don't understand and no one ever will how vital it is
that soon this whole table will darken and be forgotten
while we sit and walk around elsewhere there is no cause for alarm
kindly get on with your work but nevertheless something is coming
out of the sky into the open air we so rarely inhabit it falls down
across the wooden huts and pine trees across the electric toasters half
the radiators in London spring into life once more and people
are standing on carpets murdering truth. Which recovers.
With some help and isn't that up to us? Isn't this
what is left of twenty-seven cosmologies while the reels and wheels
grind over and on and I'm far too busy to be important –
call out the dogs, call out the entire office,
forward and upwards to life in the crystal blocks.

In a German Car-park

I trust in the heart-work it becomes
a steady and calm series like adding
the alphabet together, thick stones and
thin stones one after another,
the avenue, the planes.

For the words spoken among us
are still cooling in the sky

And the lights go out
letter by letter
each claim dies
as day folds in.

Black windows, and the depot lamp.
And, really, not such a big night,
not so strong and not so dangerous
hardly worth traducing, leave it
alone. It works its own passage.

Night of thieves and military acts,
we are parked here. Lines scored
on the concrete simulating stonework,
fooling no one. Keep on adding
A to B and the world is home.

Bunker Hotel

So it should be quite easy now
or at least simple
to slide down into a whole compendium of places
all at once and remain too dazzled
to locate the route and render yourself
quite incapable and have to be carried
sometimes up ricketty stairs to where you sleep.

It's also quite exciting
staying in a hotel without windows.
You could really work here: you could
steer the whole bunker into victory.
The varieties of reflected light
suddenly seem a paltry affair to this
concrete corridor and threadbare carpet,
the tiny, empty, bar, the porter in his
alcove with his accounts. The spirits
that inform us enter through wires, we
listen with closed eyes. The rest
seems merely a promised thing, and
any person is ten times their promise.

To speak of love and point
to the nearest blank wall
and the rest is extra,
deserved, and won, but extra,
my own love of you, and you and you...

When all that was damaged was the map itself
of what lies between us.

Is This Dusseldorf or Kiel?

Is it sky or dawn? planets in the trees
I can almost hear the foliage brushing
under its vaulted courses and beyond that
lights in the kitchen opposite come on.

The room absorbs energy. The further
index: stars, blood, are carried
equally off with the cruising night
and only the real edge and sheen of
metal stirs, and patches of cloud
cross the bleached sky, as flakes of rust
fall into the garden. Denial and
praise, the cold touch of stone
at the path's edge is not now
my source of you.

So you see there is no solution, this web
of tensions is what we are going to live in,
into the future; to talk of breaking it
is to damage more than us; it is what
also we act by, and with, raising
messages to the ends of the earth holding
intact each working space. A spreading
light moves to the land's edge.

Where a ship is always waiting.

Passing Measures

Four Night Pacts

1.
Quite dark now on the
natant leaf, she is
trenchant to a slight curve
and patiently accedes
to the moated range.

2.
Across the axis
of the dark machine
he completes
his short song.
The blossom springs
ahead of day.

3.
Again you reach across
the blue-white sink
for the soap. It is
a silent life beyond
our familiars that
strikes the fear.

4.
The child sleeps, it is night
so the child sleeps. His father
dies into him, miles out
in some high-up cave
rigid with icefarm and void...

The child turns in his sleep,
his father's ruin
spins on a flickering eyelash
as justice and lifework
open the oiled gates
of a new fold.

Folded Message

All I've got is one eye and two brains
to love you with and I'm so concerned
especially at night for your peace
since the directions are uncertain
meagre and costly for two as for one
but to the tune of a progressive reluctance
we shall one day attain some kind of summit
don't you think? These are verifiable things:
that in the presence of two hundred screaming
aircraft known as 'the future' our slowly
unfolding certainties keep us upright
even in pitch dark while the alarm clock
in my chest keeps me gentle, where
would you be about now?

Grassy Lenses

But no one bears their tortion for ever.
It is always worked out in the end,
in decades of patient study, in the stroke
of a fast car into a cliff-face.

And isn't meanwhile a glorious never
to which the starry margins bend,
in decades of patient study, in the hope
of any old vehicle arriving at a meeting.

Clouds and Birds over Wolfscote

Gliding onwards, all the difficult
things of the earth, and how we re-
learn to call them. This evening
five crows move over the garden to
roost on the hill; leave it there as
much as to say that the earth
is as a matter of fact adoration
in its slightest hint of length.
Many have borne witness to this
and never known an instruction to
achieve or not make blobs and
scratches, in French écriture.
Designed to omit almost everything
we do if a hand can touch with such
sweeping gentility the upper of
any known thing.
                    Omitting to mention
our ungainliness against
the possible gain.

Boletus under Narrowdale

Or only that it is worth writing
for no eyes to see and as dully and
imageless as it comes (like a swallow
between the rustling and complaining
roots of our patience) as
flat as that, that living furthers.

Prelude

Snow has settled in the lines
Of an old ridge-and-furrow system
Striping the gently sloping dark
Green fields, engrossed script
Of duration, repetition, authority
At which that calm baby in the self
That finds it so difficult to speak
Lowers an eyelid on the shrinking day
And suddenly says outright
The entire brochure of love and all.
Stay here before you fall.

Further Education

Ah, to be a full citizen of here, the nation
Of sheer being, the real that fits like a glove.
So where is the pass? I turned on Radio One
And an elderly man was speaking of a personal love
Which had sustained him through an entire life,
Moving a constant gratefulness between him and his wife.
I had to acknowledge my unworthiness of such emotion
And I asked why or how a resistance came upon us
Implanting a resentment when the tie is from above
And we can't speak so warmly as he. But trust
Also in a working fate we bear together, and when
The ward light blinks for one the other will gasp for certain.
And at variance become more richly equal and when
The pulse breaks for one the other will grasp for the curtain.

Poem Beginning with a Line by Nicholas Moore

Oh buzzing bee, art is a thing of love / as love
Is a thing of art, they build each other. But who knows who
Is the contract salesman and who is the perfect lover?
'It is what the girl wears that makes her beautiful'
It is what she brings, cattle, solid gold rings, a promise
Consolidated over centuries, of which it is full
As the river is full of sky. Not the slightest threat
To the self is implied or taken. Richly the promise is met
Richly the table is spread and the insects forced into retreat,
The pickers and snatchers rigorously excluded from a slow
Tableau where generosity is the defining percept of the other.
And this ring we carry on our bodies as we buzz round ever after
And the foul dry winds suck the pools and harden the skin but we try
To maintain our patent purpose. If there were only love it would die.

Bole Hill

Who is it comes knocking at my door in the night
Breaking the quiet darkness, calling me out? –
Brother, colleague, I am the world's dimmest lout,
Why do you want me out there in the source of light
What use am I to the nascent day? And he says
He has been sent from corners of the land
To gather solidarity to a scattered band
Of true souls, thinkers sweeping in a maze
Of brutality and he says the world is badly
Balanced on a point of trust, he says the whole
World is an unstable thing, a shrinking caul
On truth and we have to meet love's demand.
In the darkness the rain falls from leaf
To leaf and beats upon the ground.

Little Bolehill

The stack of days is useless, there's nothing,
The days are nothing in the pocket no books
On the shelf: a white wall and a black kettle.
You can think & feel freely but there is nothing
Left of the day to have or write into a book
Or stack away, finally only a cup and a kettle
That we take with us into the garden where nothing
Grows except statues and ideas or sometimes books
But a real enough garden with leaves. Put the kettle
On the brick-lined hearth to simmer as the book
Says and pour slowly, hot water on the leaves.
Perhaps it is a life's richer act to wish nothing
Further than its creation out of nothing
Of a real and final thing as true as leaves.

Midsummer Common

What were the victory fireworks like in 1945
If you didn't believe in the war but loved
The people and their victory? The sky
Scripted in hot lights, the sky full,
And veiled rim to rim. Oh to escape
Under the edge of night, red hair streaming
In the wind like coals in a world fire, a fire
To heat the world's best wishes to a red
Glowing ardour, the great ring on the bone
And purpose of love for the field is full
Of folk, firework, seedscape. And return
As a soldier returns, to what? There is something
Further out in the dark than the painted stars,
Something that also hates us and our wars.

Dublin

Venus is shrouded and the dark houses
Contradict life which contradicts itself
In a mass of talk through a bar doorway.
It fades, white moon, white statue against
Black wall, cut of equity. Canal moon
Floating in fuzz under Ballybough Road
Corridor of glow between cliff houses
Leading surely to the end of itself
And a drunken cripple in a doorway
Sings his Irish heart out as if all the
Gardens of memory lost in the moon
Could lay this mist and clear this cruel code.
Suddenly I was a red horseman
Helping a blind man to cross the road.

Loft

I was resting quietly in my slight knowledge,
Barely support enough to any human freight
Through the world and the clouds! the clouds
Shooting across the dark sky for as soon
As we notice the clouds moving the edge of
Our tenure starts to erode, they skate past
And we're suspended in the bounds of a cosmic
Sandwich, something God planned for lunch.
And I am far too sober to confront that great
Display of uncaring with a wedge of unique
Script – which is what it takes, mounted
From the very rooftops, beaming in state:
That when it comes to the bite (calmly) we seek
Further than cloud, appetite uncounted.

Hackney Loft

The clouds, yes the clouds shoot
Under the sky brown with town light
Bearing our purpose away across
The horizon as if it doesn't matter
And what can we bring against it
But a darker hedge of thought,
Rain, mass, burning coal.

Or a saffron headband, mute
While it lasts, fading light
Consumed in the street: the loss
Of our years doesn't much matter
If the day is brought out fit
To die as indeed it should.
Hail, heart, decisive goal.

Parker's Piece

What were the victory fireworks like in 1945
If you didn't believe in the war but loved
The people and their victory? Hoping perhaps
These would be the last bangs, this the last
Time the sky was shot with fire and the man
With red hair find his rest at length,
Lying like evening on the earth, alive
And achieved, at full, like flowers, like red
Tulips in full bloom and begin to lapse
Openly back into history, a dark green bed.
What reason is there why each and every one
Shouldn't inhabit a working peace that ends
Separately, as we carry our peculiar fates
Forwards through the smouldering gates.

Passing Measures

S. Cecilia in Trastevere

What moves between bright thoughts and finished body?
Music's idea turns in the clouds and she
Lies on the floor, denied her time, face
Turned away so as not to see her own pain...

What moves between is all we live, heavy
And light, banked in winged tiers, that we
Carve our eyes through day by day, kiss
The bed and back to the devastating sight again.

I believe in a centre to the wasted life
That is carried before the world and holds love
Through distance and strife to the end of a
Perfect reconciliation however many times
Occluded in failed responses finally standing
Whole and obvious, like an orchard in the rain.

S. Maria in Trastevere

Final beings in a golden field, ravenous concavity,
Glowing up there in the darkness, impossible promise
Sucking our very breath to their eyes, every single thing
That's worth a thought burning away and there it is.

So we have it as we don't and wish it as we
Tear it apart and suffer the weight of
Inhabited light on our dark stinging
Eyes at the sudden cancellation of hope.

I wander in the darkened city thinking
I know no purpose to this thread of being
Or where it shall come to an end. The shops
And taverns gleam to the side of the way,
The central distance stays empty until that
Lucent shield cuts it clean, I hope it is.

S. Pietro in Montorio

Dust, road, flying leaf. Deny
Any perfection which is not made, which
Curves not back to hold mental heat
To the dark ground the bright stone.

It is all burning chaos, it all wastes
Force to suck nothings to a point except
That one grace we own and are, to meet
Cosmic dispersal at a still, equal, dome.

I stand in my absence in front of a thing
That stands in its presence and fits it
To perfection. The city is a tensed fixture
Behind me as far as the eye can want to see.
The sky curves less kindly, the planets greet
Less formally the pitted world than this crown.

Djebel Bou Dabbous

Shepherds like posts, with little ragged flocks
Of brown goats, over the plains as the sun arcs
Across the sky from one side to the other
They stand there like statues in parks,
That stillness, 'where even today a god might enter
And not be diminished'.

The shepherds' heads are full of Arabic,
Prayers, curses, calculation, save and stitch
Like all of us. Heads full of breathing.
The only god space I know is made in script
As a rich hollow at the heart of meaning
That can't be finished

And finishes us, shepherds, poets, freaks,
Persons of the people set to watch
The frail resource. We signal like brothers
Across the plains and run our longings
Into musical continua as the hawks hover
Over all we mean, guarding our edge.

Djebel Bou Dabbous

Of what are we ashamed? We are still enough
In a world made daily more expensive. We stop
The car and take out a blanket and spread
A cloth on the ground. We have cheese and biscuits
Figs and mineral water, we share them together.
A feathery breeze touches our heads

Like an idea of completion: acts that pass
Well into the world beyond our short and
Faltering lives, acts of trust in sudden
Fits of star-hurt and deathly patience
Claiming nothing but the limits of a tongue we
Openly declare, small in the peaceful deserts.

And all round us as we sit there in the puff
Of wind small flocks of brown sheep stand
Quietly browsing across the long plain
Of thin grass, with their masters. Mes petits,
We are ashamed to be alone. O my gossips,
The god hollow throbs and hurts.

Ghar El Melh

The light that sits on the edge of the leaf
In the gardens by the sea without limit,
The words on the ground crisp with response

Again and again from item to item it shines
across the road and out to the harbour's white wall
open by line to distance, unwilling to domesticate.

Real gardens by the sea, growing vegetables
and fishermen camped in reed huts, riding
social injustice like a big wave: with glee.

The white houses wedged into the cliff top,
the sky wedge focused on the ear, that hears
dominion on the wire and shudders. For the world

Is a house too big too small, harm is laid
into the closed square but the streets end
suddenly in the grey dust where no one lives

And tracks turn down to the sea gardens at day's
length, brightness blazing across, continuing
to shed acute definition you love-torn spheres.

Leaving me to think that the mind's track on
soul-light is instrumental to the earth's
equilibrium, as I have grown older.

Saint Séverin's Maze

I can't wait to get out in the night crowds,
And I do, sharp-eyed I weave the streets.

Un sandwich grecque at the corner, this is
The bright capital full of people, this is

Why.
And a slow Chinese cake.

Suddenly the lit zone ends, I am lost
Among stone walls, look up and the sky

Is writing a thesis in manganese dioxide
At the closing of the gates.

Something fine, all dangers past,
Turns me home. Something not-fine bars the way.

There are people sleeping on the pavement in the rain.
The water runs off their backs into the gutter.

Causeway

I defy your bloody language. I cast
My whole life at your delay. My lapses from care
Are a perpetual night surrounding my mind.

Pascal's Corner

When does the society of solitude give space
Even to its own history? The dark and quiet back
Street. I stop at a small wine shop I remember
From six years ago and again buy one cheap
Rather unusual bottle and clutching it walk on,
The long boulevard past the prison, the hospital,
The observatory, shadowed by approaching night.

> City walls at the threshold of script
> Hard as the space that hardens round
> The heart since there is no help,
> That has worn us since flesh began
> To make way for death. Until we turn
> To the wall's door and angrily cast
> Our whole lives at this dark delay.

Darkness falls from the sky, leaving it
Light, above the long boulevard. On the
Left the prison wall called Health, to the
Right among trees a hospital called Grace
And further on the observatory where we turn
Against everything we know in our haste
To love. Hill and valley echo with delight.

Street and station say it is all right.

Bolehill

I shall never forget the grove
and the grassy mounds

I shall never forget you
fighting me on a pillow

I cannot thank you enough, when
the snow came

It melted (when our
tears came they

Hardened)
and ran down the fields.

Hastings

The time remains
in which we were virtuous

Everything else has vanished
It doesn't matter

How little remains – the soul,
a tiny part of the body

And there were cats in the window.

Irish Drones

All those chanters
all faring well enough

And along he comes, what's
his name, Willie Clancie, Billy

Pigg, not Irish either and
plays as if

His heart's cut in two.
It isn't. Somebody's is.

Maybe it's mine, the
listener, maybe it's us.

The as if
is a long acquaintance with the sky.

Golden Slumbers

To have you I would bar the fields
and turn the ores into the stream

I would occupy the eyrie of my failure
far into the night night after night

Until the ancestral bones
formed a nest for my patience

In which I would sit and couple the numbers
of my life without regret

And remember with uncertainty the world

In which we were and not, all
our loves in vain.

***

No love is in vain,
reader.

Vallée de la Vézère

Here I set my suitcase down and
Swear by the twin stars that
Triangulate our wars the new
Meadows open their doors at
Evening's end the soft sand
Slides along the river bed
The singing night birds
Plunge their beaks into comfort

And drain it thus and thus. War
Leans on the shadow's edge
Where light pours into the ground
And slides through caves, the star
On the sole against suicide
And anger signed at *bouches d'ombres*,
Please, anger locked lightless.
I open my suitcase looking for a ring.

Glow Worm True Worm

Bright hyphen in the dark valley
Between the path and the river
I never even tried, the water slips
Sideways and the little owls hop
From branch to branch in the dark,
Living like us with what they aren't
And never will be, and the stars
Pulse dryly to themselves, a steady and
Irrevocable calling across the poles
Across the warehouses and sorting
Offices across the merely possible the
Synapse fires as if suddenly us.
But I always thought love was deserved,
I thought it was the earth shining.

Heinrich Biber

Passion's cloak, passion's three-step
And you're there. If you're there
Be there, show pluck, walk in the
Streets of Laredo head high, danger
On the cuff and mortal precept.
Willing, I mean, to die for nothing
Since we do and have plenty of time.
In this light I couldn't
Love you more and scratch an elk on
The cave wall in five minutes flat
Because passion creates what it means
Out of thin air in red streams. And turn
To the bank as the moon shrinks
And the membrane tightens across
The mossy fields, the débris of our
Gain signed in passionless lymph.
Take your partner, harmonious nymph
And treacle the earth without blame.
Out of my case I choose a clear name.

Magdelanian

Hand stencils on concave surfaces at the fearful threshold. Hollow
horses and bulging bovines: desire, that claim on light between mouth
and legs crashes day by day against the lens, it really is too late to
'phone. The last signature is set at *bouches d'ombres*: thresholds of lower
galeries containing running water, doors into the world's black fall. A
headless snake on the banks of the underground river, management
moves in the night in the dark back streets in the flashed message while
everyone's sleep, relentless laceration of the unnamed and homeless.
Speech blocked, broken membrane, casual and arbitrary death in a war
for want of better. We cost it all in poetry, wild notes in our dark
mouths and the animals alongside, stacked red on black, small
flickering shades on the walls of the river, phosphenes in attendance
overhead.

In Manus Tuas

for John Sheppard

Gendering touch that gathers
and cups like a boat on the
rotting sea because I tendered

All I am to your safety. So we are eye
to eye, heart to purpose, bent
forward in the western wind

That blows over the hard and
blanched ground towards an idea
of work as shelter.

The children raised there will blow
this distance to anthills, and hand
themselves to aerials

And hunt themselves to equity
in an undertree light loud with one
mutual cry – of succession

Dying to a rich suture of the future.
Deep then in the oily mulch a
smouldering hope, a patient ear

To another's woe and a door behind the snow.
How it seals the film of spring,
where we ride forth in company.

* * *

for Syd Barrett

Voiced consonants buzzing through Suffolk
to a dark road white houses when I
knew the cost I had no language,

My death spread over the fens, love
predicates a real future or
burns to nothing like a white leaf.

My hands felt like two balloons. Did you
yes you did, see the great flocks
of Scandinavian wood pigeons and

Plovers on the ploughed fields, hundreds, in
slowly dimming winter light wearing
a question to be proud of, bending

To the day's end calling where is the
river where is the course of us
where is the bridge of flesh?

Not here, or worth knowing
in a society that reckons care
by tenths. The sheen of their wings

Makes a sea of the field
and a person's age is a grateful fact
sailing out in it with you

Sitting in the car in a dark road white
houses bookshop open answer closed
fruitful company in a closing world.

I have to believe what the earth so
distinctly says. Settle noisily honourable birds
onto everyone's food.

Do It Again

It's automatic when I
Talk to old friends the
Conversation turns to
Girls we knew when their
Hair was soft and

whiter than star
heavier than sea

death white as glass
pass over me

Well I've been thinkin bout
All the places All the faces we
Missed and then

Bar Carol

for Schubert

There are worse deaths than singing,
worse singings than death's.
Gently over black ever

Shifting water the wooden craft
Moves out. The newspaper
soaked in itself, sinks.

And the city, there, circles scripted
over the sea articulating light we
adore by rote, and touched in the

Tainted fall of socialistic promises
like petals of death sign out
with a blown shrug. The city divides

And sheds but the world waits for ever
the great curve of thought we
slowly sail round towards singing.

* * *

for Jack Yeats

And love alone, untouched by ideology,
is a rare thing that the flesh
calls out and runs to meet. There they
stand, hand in hand, watching the horses
pounding the green field at the sea's edge,
green pulse at the street's end, always and
precisely that sundering coil of breath.

And love alone, without bonus, roars
in my ear the final score. Wherever on
earth you both are or not, in that time and
measure left me I wouldn't dream or
anything but honour. And silly too,
forgetting the exact ground whereon those
two eyes bought my breath.

And love aligns the bruised letters offering
nothing to the future but itself what it
purely earns. Snow brushing the hill,
honesty of the offered arm, daybreak
over the ruins of will. So the earth
lightens to a hawk's point and a silver
cup for the loser, as ever was.
Take it this parting prize this blow.

Prelude: Night Shift

Where there are lights there are people,
In a hospital ward at night, shifting
And groaning, talking quietly not to
Wake others, switching on and off
A dim light over the door: from outside
A flicker in the window as the pedestrian
Passes under the tall building in the middle
Of the night, walking steadily home
To light a candle and carry it up to bed.

Where there's a light the mind is in question.
There are thousands, across the city,
Cross-shifting lights of which any at
Some time serves to tell, to guide
Someone to somewhere, the nearest
Toilet or out into the soaring arcs.
The pedestrian lies in the bleak loft,
His light by a cup of water on a bed-
side chair, reaching for a page about eyes.

The night sky opens and shuts cloud-curtains
On the theatre of everything we aren't. They stream
To the horizon as the shepherd in the play
Calls his cares back and the flashing machine
Cones to a final top. There the greatest distance
Is absolute contact. And the watch lights
Gather quietly for the last time round one
Who dies before dawn to prove
That time sets all things right.

Oh My Beauty!

At some point of a life
An arm goes over a shoulder.
Then we know what we are.
A helpless wish, a wishful help,
The best of what we are.
The city rears to a heraldry
And the stars fall to the side.

The sky reaches over
A mind or shoulder
To yellow meadows and brown
Hills where strife is over and the city
Falls to a market. The stars
Lie in the grass like twists of bestness
Spelling Time Sets All Things Right.

Men of Destiny

Walking into the nation bearing
The sun in their lineaments blood
And salt on the ground everything
As it actually is.

Pure light stinking to heaven
From a mental rib-cage the ever
Wanted in the moment of decision,
Birth-shattering gender.

Then proudly forth, star on the ground,
Frail vehicle chained to the
Compass wound saying Men it is Men
not Time sets all things right.

The Stolen Picture

Men, if only they would. The woman
Casts a small pink rose

Across the blue morning, we speak
At last of the world

And it is too late it is fallen and lost.
Time brings lost things back.

The Little Watercolour at Sligo

The point of pain
At which the voice either
Cracks or cruises. The little fat man

Makes it, whoever he is, drunk but
Not too drunk in village night his
Mouth like a typographical O he

Stops to sing, his head rises, his
Arms fall, and it works: he
Cruises, out across time

Nameless and small, he
Sails a stranger's psyche, saying
Cast your (care) crown. This

Is success, this is being, this
Is where love fastens us to the earth
And time sees to the rest.

That Grand Conversation Was Under the Rose

The person in his/her moment supreme.
Of the successions of which history is the sum.
So the grand conversation can start. Art
And poetry and all their costly trappings
Immediately vanish for ever — there's plenty
Of time, no one's making a recording, sit down
Here and be the failure your heart's ease knows.
Don't be modern, don't be threatened,
Be just, be welcome and be kindly and the earth
Is yours for the duration. The stage is set
Because the heart is in need, adverbs and
Prepositions everywhere begging to be used.
Like the surface of the earth rolling into itself

We know and have always known what this
Gift is for, placed on our lips. It is for
Time's reconciliation. It is for eloquent farewells
And that grand conversation under the rose.

Part I
Lines on the Liver. Ferry Press 1981
Tracks and Mineshafts. Grosseteste Press 1983

Part II
Sea Watches. Prest Roots Press 1991
Sea Watch Elegies. Poetical Histories 1993
Between Harbours. Artist's book by Colin Whitworth, Cambridge 1996

Part III
Ospita. Poetical Histories 1987. Reprinted in *The New British Poetry*, Paladin 1988, and in *Contemporary Criticism* 19, 1997.

Part IV
Noon Province. Poetical Histories 1989. Second edition in *Noon Province et autres poèmes*, Atelier La Feugraie (France) 1996

Part V
Love-Strife Machine. Ferry Press 1969
The Canterbury Experimental Weekend. Arc 1971
The Linear Journal. Grosseteste Press 1973
Untitled Sequence. Wild Honey Press (Ireland) 2000
Snow has Settled… Bury Me Here. Shearsman Books 1997
(trilogy) {
 Reader. 1992
 Lecture. Equipage 1993
 Author. Folio (Salt) 1998

Books of poetry not drawn on for this collection:

Strange Family. Burning Deck Press (USA) 1973
The Musicians The Instruments. Many Press 1978
Preparations. Curiously Strong Press 1979
Royal Signals. Short Run Press 1995
Distant Points. Reality Street Editions 1995
Alstonefield. Oasis Books and Shearsman Books 1995
Hilltop Episode. Shearsman #41, 1999

Grateful acknowledgement is made to the editors and publishers of all these items, who went to so much trouble on my behalf, especially Andrew Crozier, Tim Longville, and Tony Frazer: heroes of the 'small-press scene'.